Lessons from the Ocean

By Donalyn Knight

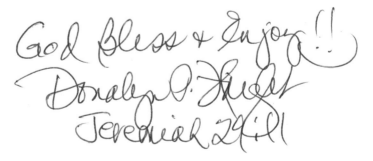

God Bless & Enjoy!!

Donalyn O. Knight

Jeremiah 29:11

Xulon
PRESS

LESSONS From The OCEAN
God's Blessings and Promises Revealed Through Seashells and The Ocean
by Donalyn P Knight

Printed in the United States of America

ISBN 9781625090126

www.xulonpress.com

DEDICATION

My Lord and Savior Jesus Christ

My Mother, Margaret Knight for her unwavering love, friendship and encouragement and for leading me into a personal relationship with Jesus at a younger age and for being that example of a Godly mother- I love you, Mama

My Dear Friend Patti Angel for encouraging me to write these thoughts down so they can be shared with others

My Dear Family and Friends whose love, friendship and encouragement throughout the years makes me truly thankful to God for blessing me with the most wonderful family and friends I could ever be blessed with- I am rich indeed because of them! Thank You Jesus!

Shells come in many shapes, sizes and colors – they're all creations of God and they all have value.

All of the shells had a job to do in protecting something.

The broken ones are no less important than those intact.

Too often, we just want the "pretty ones".

Shells – even the delicate ones – travel great distance at times and overcome wind and waves to make it to shore.

When I search for shells, I have to take what the ocean gives me to choose from — as in life, we must deal with what is handed to us.

Sometimes God allows us to see something big ahead, but as we head toward it and reach that spot, He will direct us to something even more incredible – He allowed us to see in part as He knew we would not be able to see the "big picture" until we reached a certain point in our walk.

Sometimes something totally unexpected washes ashore – a treasure unto itself . . . . . a delightful blessing.

You never know what's going to wash up next – that's the beauty of perseverance. . . . .

There is a certain rhythm to the ocean – as there is in life.

. . . . . .There is also a "season" for things – shells, birds, tides, etc. . . .that is, certain types of shells wash up certain times of the year; birds migrate at certain times of the year. . . . . . .

What looks good on one side of the shell can be crumbled underneath – like people – they may look great on the outside, but . . . .

Sometimes beauty gets tangled up in seaweeds and is missed. We get tangled up in the "seaweeds" of life and that keeps our light from shining because we're buried under "stuff".

What you can't see CAN hurt you – i.e. jellyfish and other things hidden under the water. . . . .

When the tide washes over the shells, they come clean, just like when Jesus "washes" our sins away, we become clean . . . .

Over time, layers of "stuff" can smother us and our beauty is hidden; however, the beauty is Still there. . . . .

As the beach builds up its layers on the beach, we build our foundation on the "Rock". . . . . . .

As the colors of the shells sparkle in the sun, when the "SON" is shining through us, our true "colors" come out . . . . . .

. . . . .When the "Son" isn't shining through us, it's still there – just harder to see. He didn't move – we did . . . . .and the beauty is not as evident. . . . .

Shells are tough; shells are durable; shells can weather the storms. . . . .and so can we. . . . .

Resistance makes shells strong and beautiful – from the pounding of the waves to the cutting of the sand . . . . .as it is with us, Jesus is the Potter; we are the clay. . . . . .He makes us into something beautiful. . . . . . .

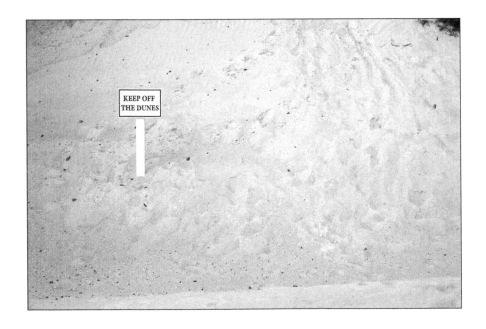

Though things can "erode", they can be build back over time. . . . . . .

The waves carry the fragile shells and gently deposit them on shore – just as Jesus carries us through the hard times, brings us through the hard times, brings us through and gently deposits us back into the flow of life. . . . .

When I've watched the sea gulls get after each other. . . . . .I now understand the meanings of "feathers ruffled", "henpecked" and how they "tune out" the others squawking. . . . .

When Jesus "washes" our sins away, we can more clearly see the beauty of all that He has in store for us. . . . .

Don't be so worried about what's ahead that you overlook what's right in front of you. . . . . .

You don't have to be perfect to be pretty. . . . .

With the "Son" behind you, you can see more clearly how He lights the Way. . . . . .

A knowledge of what's out there – (sharks, jellyfish, rip tides, etc.) can protect you – if you'll pay attention. . . . .

When the storms come and the waves "crash" the shore, those who have "deep roots" can withstand the pressure and the pounding . . . . . .

A fish out of water dies; apart from the Living Water, we die. . . . .

. . . . .so glad that God doesn't choose us like we choose our shells. . . .

As in Windsurfing – you ride best with the "Wind" (power and presence of God) behind you. . . . .

In these uncertain and "churning" times, the more we know about what God's Word says and what He promises, the more at peace – like the still of the ocean – we'll be . . . .

. . . . . .like the more you know about the power of the ocean, the more at ease you are around it. . . . . .

He's already told us these things Ahead of time so that we would Know and Not fear. . . .Hebrews 2:13. . . . . .

When the birds migrate to the Florida shore, they just "seem" to know when to go and where to go. . . .so should it be in our relationship to the Lord – we don't always need to try to take things into our own hands. Go TO Him and allow Him to show us. . . . .

No matter how Dark the ocean, how much fury it may release – it is Still the ocean in all of its majesty – as God is Still God – He is Still Holy. . . . .

God equipped all of the "sea" birds so as not to let any go hungry —
some can scurry faster; some have longer beaks; some can fly faster
and farther; think smarter — so everyone has an equal chance at survival
. . . . . .if we'll use our God-given talents — not what others possess,
what We possess — there will be an abundance for us as well. . . . .

When we're "focused" we can see obstacles sooner and thereby overcome them faster. . . . .

A trained "eye" spots certain shells quickly just as a trained "spiritual eye" can discern things easier. . . . .

So many people pass by and don't even stop to admire the beauty of the ocean as they're walking down the beach – they're so busy talking and thinking of everything they have to do; just as at times, we seem too busy for God – how that must sadden Him!. . . . .He has So much to share with us and to give us, yet we're too wrapped up with "stuff" to notice. . . . .

Sometimes we run to snatch a beautiful shell from the tide before the ocean sucks it back in – the same way God reaches down and "snatches" us from a bad situation before we get caught in the flow and taken out to sea. . . . .

The birds "face" the wind – they know what allows them to soar – they know where their Lift comes from . . . . .Likewise, we should be facing the "Son" – that's where our Lift comes from and allows us to Soar. . . . .

See by the tracks in the sand – where will yours lead on the beach of life?. . . . .

The sandpipers "flirt" with the edge of the waves — scurrying so as to never be overtaken by them, we must be careful that we don't "flirt" with sin — if we get too close, we'll be overtaken and swept away. . . . .

God Knows His children just as I know certain shells – I can quickly recognize them because of their characteristics and qualities – He know us inside and out. . . . .

Sand castles?. . . . . . .Build yours on the "Rock" that will not be shaken. . . . .

"Seek and ye shall find" . . . . – the shells will not come knocking at your door . . . . . .Go seek; always remember, God's promises do not return void!. . . . .

Walking down the beach I noticed several run-outs. As I reached down to pick up a shell caught in the run-out, I realized that the pressure of the water was pushing the shell deeper and deeper into the "rut". . . . It's like when we're in a rut, the pressures of life try to keep us down, but if we reach out to the Lord, He will lift us out of that and put us "back into the flow" of life. . . . .

The deafening roar of the ocean can drown out the voices . . . . . .at times, all of the "Noise" around us drowns out the call of God. . . . .

Notice the resistance of the shells as the water rushes around it — Nothing is more powerful than God's Word, so though the world may try to sweep you away, stand firm on God's Promises and principles. He keeps His promises and you Will Not be disappointed!!!!. . . . . .

When searching for shells one needs to follow the "shell line" of which there are often 2,3,4 of them depending on where the last tide stopped. If we walk between the lines . . . .that is, down the middle of the road, we're going to miss all of the treasures and splendor of what the ocean deposited, because we weren't staying close to where we could see and experience the joy of "the Treasure". . . .such is the case with Christ in our lives – we want to stay close to Him to experience that joy!

Walk on purpose, breathe on purpose, live on purpose – take in the day that God has given!. . . . . . .

Each shell has characteristics and coloring unto itself that sets it apart from every other shell – How do you want to be identified? What do you want your legacy to be?. . . . .

Ever notice how the pelicans follow their leader? Who do you follow?. . . . .

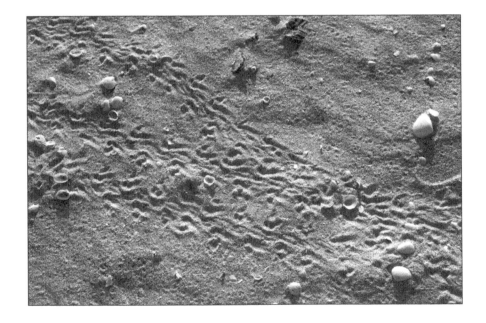

The turtle patrol. . . . .sold out to their cause-up at the crack of dawn patrolling-eagerly looking for signs of turtle nesting; marking the spot; doing everything humanly possible to protect them. . . .ohhh, if we could just look after each other with that same energy and enthusiasm, and better yet-seek God with that kind of fervor – what a better world this would be!. . . . .

I noticed on my walks at the beach that there was always a spot in front of my dear friend Robin's house where I would always find a very special shell. It totally blew my mind as it became apparent over time that this was not a coincidence. I believe that signified the love of God through my friend, her mother and her family that I am so blessed to know and hold dear in my heart. . . . .Thank You God!

The sand crabs – they scurry about knowing they've always go a safe place to hide from danger. . . . .Where's your safe place? The arms of Jesus?. . . . . . .

Sandrifts can smother us and cover us – "smothered" by the world – it doesn't have to be that way, though. . . . .We have a Savior who can dig us out of anything!. . . . .

During a storm the beach gets pounded by the surf; however, the storms are but for a short time and then the "good" weather returns. That reminds us that in the "storms" of life, if we'll just hold on and keep the faith, the "good" weather will return . . . .

I was taught from a young age to look for the dolphins - a sign of safe water . . . . . .and so it is with Our Father – Look for Him – He is our Safe Water. . . . . . .

The salt lines on the shore show how far the water got . . . . .where will you leave your mark? Your legacy? Your love for the Lord?. . . . . . .

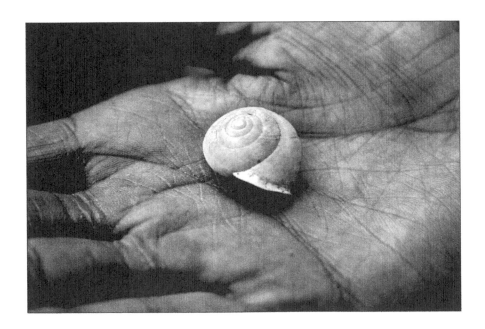

Walking down the beach, I had already collected some beautiful shells in my hand and was trying hard to "protect" them as I was far away from my destination. Throughout the journey, I juggled them at times, trying not to drop them or crush them in any way so they would make it safely to their destination for all to enjoy. I believe God gives us special "gifts" to protect and handle carefully so we can use them for His glory. . . . .everything is His and comes From Him. . . .take care.

I was watching a father teaching his young son to surf . . . . .the boy got up on the board and away he went, only to come crashing down through the waves. As the boy stood there shocked and crying, the father came running, hugged him and consoled him, and I'm sure gave a little instruction. Within a few seconds the father guided the boy back out to try again. . . . . .Our Father does that with us – He picks us up when we fall and encourages us to get back out there and get back on the "surf board" of life.

To God Be the Glory! I Love You, Jesus!

CPSIA information can be obtained at www.ICGtesting.com
Printed in the USA
LVOW04s0055011014

406590LV00003B/3/P

9 781625 090126